Wadeable Stream Monitoring in Allegheny Portage Railroad National Historic Site, Delaware Water Gap National Recreation Area, Johnstown Flood National Memorial, and Upper Delaware Scenic and Recreational River:

Eastern Rivers and Mountains Network 2010 Summary Report

Natural Resource Data Series NPS/ERMN/NRDS—2011/212

Caleb J. Tzilkowski, Andrew S. Weber, Kristina K. Callahan, and Matthew R. Marshall

National Park Service
Northeast Region
Eastern Rivers and Mountains Network
Forest Resources Building
University Park, PA 16802

December 2011

U.S. Department of the Interior
National Park Service
Natural Resource Stewardship and Science
Fort Collins, Colorado

The National Park Service, Natural Resource Stewardship and Science office in Fort Collins, Colorado publishes a range of reports that address natural resource topics of interest and applicability to a broad audience in the National Park Service and others in natural resource management, including scientists, conservation and environmental constituencies, and the public.

The Natural Resource Data Series is intended for timely release of basic data sets and data summaries. Care has been taken to assure accuracy of raw data values, but a thorough analysis and interpretation of the data has not been completed. Consequently, the initial analyses of data in this report are provisional and subject to change.

All manuscripts in the series receive the appropriate level of peer review to ensure that the information is scientifically credible, technically accurate, appropriately written for the intended audience, and designed and published in a professional manner. Data in this report were collected and analyzed using methods based on established, peer-reviewed protocols and were analyzed and interpreted within the guidelines of the protocols.

Views, statements, findings, conclusions, recommendations, and data in this report do not necessarily reflect views and policies of the National Park Service, U.S. Department of the Interior. Mention of trade names or commercial products does not constitute endorsement or recommendation for use by the U.S. Government.

This report is available from the Eastern Rivers and Mountains Network website (http://science.nature.nps.gov/im/units/ERMN) and the Natural Resource Publications Management website (http://www.nature.nps.gov/publications/NRPM).

Please cite this publication as:

NPS 423/111731, 620/111731, 427/111731, 647/111731, December 2011

Contents

Figures

Tables

Appendixes

Acknowledgments

The Eastern Rivers and Mountains Network (ERMN) is grateful for the cooperation and support from all parks in the network. Without the logistical support, housing, and knowledge provided by the parks, the ERMN could not sustain Vital Signs monitoring at the current level.

Acronyms

BCP	Boundary control point
BMI	Benthic macroinvertebrate
DO	Dissolved oxygen
EPA	United States Environmental Protection Agency
ERMN	Eastern Rivers and Mountains Network
IDAS	Invertebrate Data Analysis System
MAHR	Mid-Atlantic Highlands Region
MIBI	Multimetric Index of Biotic Integrity
MTI	Macroinvertebrate Tolerance Index
NHS	National Historic Site
NMem	National Memorial
NPS	National Park Service
NRA	National Recreation Area
RTH	Richest targeted habitat
SRMP	Scenic Rivers Monitoring Program
SRR	Scenic and Recreational River
UNT	Unnamed tributary
USGS	United States Geological Survey

Executive Summary

The mission of the National Park Service (NPS) is "to conserve unimpaired the natural and cultural resources and values of the national park system for the enjoyment of this and future generations." To help support its mission, and as a result of the Natural Resource Challenge, more than 270 parks in the national park system were organized into 32 Inventory and Monitoring Networks to implement a sustained and scientifically defensible natural resource monitoring program (NPS 1999). One of those networks, the Eastern Rivers and Mountains Network (ERMN), includes nine parks in New Jersey, New York, Pennsylvania, and West Virginia.

The NPS' purpose for natural resource monitoring is to determine the status and trends in the condition of selected park resources (Fancy et al. 2009). Monitoring 13 ecological vital signs throughout the ERMN is expected to provide early warning of impending threats and provide a basis for understanding and identifying meaningful change in natural systems characterized by complexity, variability, and surprises (Marshall and Piekielek 2007). Furthermore, vital signs are expected to provide the ability to assess the efficacy of management and restoration efforts (NPS 2008).

During 2008, the ERMN began collecting data using the Wadeable Streams Monitoring Protocol, which addressed the benthic macroinvertebrate and water quality vital signs. This report summarizes the status of benthic macroinvertebrate communities and water quality in selected wadeable streams throughout parks in the Northern Appalachians Ecoregion of the ERMN (i.e., Allegheny Portage Railroad National Historic Site, Delaware Water Gap National Recreation Area, Johnstown Flood National Memorial, and Upper Delaware Scenic and Recreational River). Data collected since 2008 (with emphasis on data collected during 2010) are presented and discussed. All data were collected following methods detailed in the Wadeable Streams Monitoring Protocol (Tzilkowski et al. 2009).

Introduction

The mission of the National Park Service (NPS) is "to conserve unimpaired the natural and cultural resources and values of the national park system for the enjoyment of this and future generations." To help support its mission, and as a result of the Natural Resource Challenge, more than 270 parks in the national park system were organized into 32 Inventory and Monitoring (I&M) Networks to implement a sustained and scientifically defensible natural resource monitoring program (NPS 1999). One of those networks, the Eastern Rivers and Mountains Network (ERMN), includes nine parks in New Jersey, New York, Pennsylvania, and West Virginia (Figure 1).

The NPS' purpose for natural resource monitoring is to determine the status and trends in the condition of selected park resources (Fancy et al. 2009). Monitoring 13 'vital signs' (including benthic macroinvertebrates [BMI] and water quality) throughout the ERMN provides the ability to assess the efficacy of management and restoration efforts. Furthermore, vital signs are expected to provide early warning of impending threats and provide a basis for understanding and identifying meaningful change in natural systems characterized by complexity, variability, and surprises (Fancy et al. 2009). This report summarizes monitoring results of two vital signs (BMI and water quality) in four parks in the Northern Appalachians Ecoregion of the ERMN during 2010 (Table 1); additionally, data collected during 2008 and 2009 were incorporated into this report as averages of BMI metrics and water quality parameters.

A primary objective of the ERMN ecological monitoring program is to evaluate status and trends in the condition of tributary watersheds flowing into and through member parks. Watershed condition is evaluated using measures of ecosystem integrity, including streamside bird species and communities (Mattsson and Marshall 2009), forest structure and composition (Perles et al. 2009), BMI and water quality (Tzilkowski et al. 2009), and watershed land use, type, and configuration (Marshall and Piekielek 2007). Because BMI are important biological components of all but the most severely impaired streams, they are often used as indicators of ecosystem integrity. BMI are instrumental to nutrient and carbon dynamics and are an important link in stream food webs—groups that are commonly used for water quality assessment include arthropods (insects, arachnids, and crustaceans), worms, clams, and snails. Given the thorough understanding of BMI and their importance to aquatic ecosystems, they are frequently studied with regard to their responsiveness to human-induced environmental perturbations. BMI are the most frequently used organisms in water quality assessment (Carter and Resh 2001) because 1) they are relatively easy to collect, 2) many taxa can be identified to taxonomic level of family in the field (Barbour et al. 1999), and 3) several BMI life history traits (e.g., a relatively sedentary existence) make them uniquely advantageous for monitoring the condition of aquatic ecosystems.

Water chemistry and temperature strongly influence the character of aquatic ecosystems. When water quality is naturally or unnaturally altered, biotic communities and ecosystem processes are changed. Because aquatic biota are tightly linked to the physical and chemical characteristics of waters they inhabit, water quality monitoring is part of most biomonitoring programs. Surface waters throughout ERMN parks are analyzed for chemical and physical constituents, termed "core parameters," including temperature, pH, dissolved oxygen (DO), and conductivity. Monitoring BMI assemblage composition and core water quality parameters will enable the

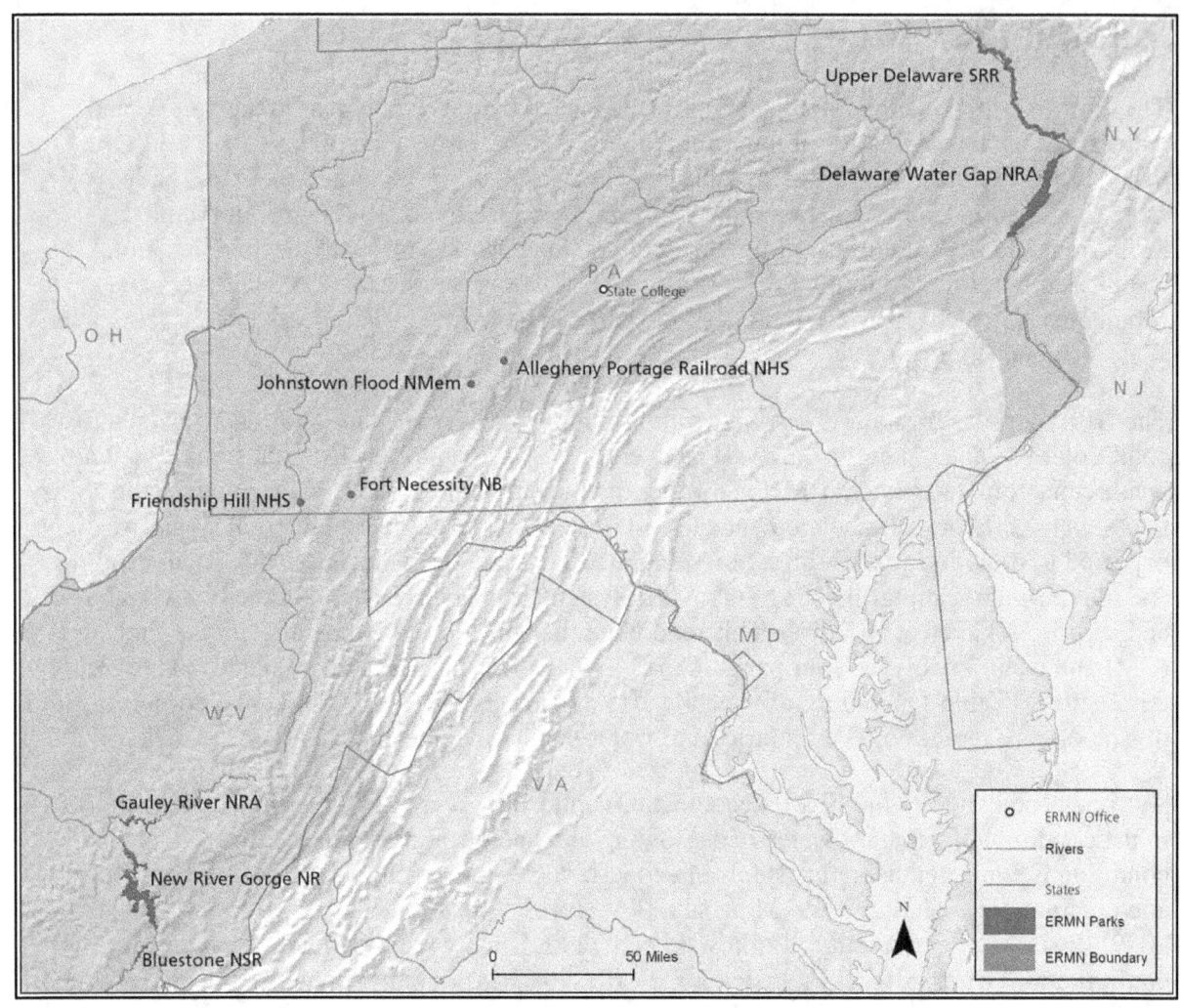

Figure 1. National parks in the Eastern Rivers and Mountains Network (ERMN).

Table 1. Number of probabilistic and targeted sampling reaches throughout 'northern' Eastern Rivers and Mountains Network parks.

Park	Probabilistic	Targeted
Allegheny Portage Railroad National Historic Site	2	1
Delaware Water Gap National Recreation Area	20	6
Johnstown Flood National Memorial	0	1
Upper Delaware Scenic and Recreational River	0	12
Total	22	20

ERMN to directly measure the characteristics of wadeable streams that are most important to the NPS mission "to conserve unimpaired the natural and cultural resources and values of the national park system for the enjoyment of this and future generations" (NPS 1999).

Objectives

The primary goal of the ERMN stream monitoring program is to collect, analyze, and report data that will help park management maintain or improve the ecological condition of wadeable streams (and rivers they are tributary to) throughout the network.

The following questions drive much of the ERMN wadeable streams monitoring program:

- What is the status and long-term trend of core water quality parameters (temperature, pH, conductivity, dissolved oxygen) in selected ERMN streams?

- What is the status and long-term trend in BMI abundance and assemblage composition in selected ERMN streams?

- Do BMI assemblages sampled within ERMN streams indicate polluted or otherwise impaired water quality?

Methods

Although a brief overview of the BMI and water quality monitoring methods is provided here, a detailed rationale of the sampling design and methods, in addition to Standard Operating Procedures, are provided in the Wadeable Stream Monitoring Protocol (Tzilkowski et al. 2009; hereafter, stream protocol).

Stream Reach Selection

The sampling units or "sites" for the stream protocol are stream reaches, which are longitudinal sections of streams, chosen to represent a uniform set of physical, chemical, and biological conditions. Reach lengths are proportional to (40×) stream widths and therefore differ among streams.

Two methods were used to select sampling reaches in the stream protocol—probabilistic (i.e., stratified-random) and targeted (i.e., non-random) approaches. The probability-based design was developed by Mattsson and Marshall (2009) for the ERMN Streamside Bird Monitoring Protocol and defined the majority of sampling reaches at Allegheny Portage Railroad National Historic Site (NHS) and Delaware Water Gap National Recreation Area (NRA; Table 1). However, it could not be used to select reaches at two parks, Johnstown Flood National Memorial (NMem) and Upper Delaware Scenic and Recreational River (SRR), primarily because all streams in these parks did not meet the requirement of having >1 km of their length within authorized park boundaries. For these parks, and for additional 'targeted' reaches in remaining parks, several factors were considered in consultation with park staff when choosing targeted sampling reaches (Tzilkowski et al. 2009). For example, many targeted reaches at Delaware Water Gap NRA and Upper Delaware SRR were selected to support the Scenic Rivers Monitoring Program (SRMP). The SRMP is an ongoing water quality monitoring program that has been jointly conducted since 1984 by the two Delaware River parks and the Delaware River Basin Commission (DRBC 2010). Collocating ERMN sampling reaches in those streams is expected to further SRMP goals, which are to: (1) assess whether existing water quality is measurably changing; (2) expand the scope of monitoring to provide an ecosystem monitoring strategy that complements baseline monitoring; and (3) provide scientific information for management decisions (DRBC 2010). In total, 22 probabilistic reaches and 20 targeted reaches were selected for monitoring throughout "northern" ERMN parks (Table 1).

Sampling Schedule

Due to a variety of factors, including the geographic distribution of network parks, regional climate and hydrologic patterns, and a field crew of two people, ERMN parks must be sampled in different seasons. The northern-most parks, which are the focus of this report, are sampled during fall, whereas southern-most parks are sampled primarily during spring.

Field Methods

Benthic macroinvertebrates were sampled using methods based on United States Geological Survey (USGS) protocols (Moulton et al. 2002) and are summarized in the stream protocol (Tzilkowski et al. 2009). BMI samples were collected from five different riffles within each reach using disturbance sampling and a slack sampler (500 μm mesh). The five discrete samples from each reach were then combined to form a composite sample (1.25 m^2 of sampled area) which was then preserved in 95% ethanol. Physical conditions (i.e., depth, flow, and substrate) were recorded at each sampling location and were as similar as possible among samples. Concurrent with BMI sampling, core water quality parameters (i.e., dissolved oxygen, pH, specific conductance, and temperature) were measured at all reaches with YSI Model 556 water quality meters (Yellow Springs Instruments Inc., Yellow Springs, OH). Reach-scale habitat conditions were assessed using U.S. Environmental Protection Agency (US EPA) methods (Barbour et al. 1999).

Laboratory Methods
Laboratory methods for processing BMI samples were based on procedures developed by the USGS (Moulton et al. 2000). A fixed-count subsample of $300\pm20\%$ individuals were sorted and identified from each sample. Generally, BMI were identified to genus using standard dichotomous keys, but some groups (e.g., Chironomidae, Oligochaeta) were identified to coarser taxonomic levels.

Data Analysis
Microsoft Access 2007 was the primary software used for storing and managing ERMN BMI and stream habitat data, whereas the Invertebrate Data Analysis System (IDAS *version 5*, USGS, Raleigh, NC) was used for resolving taxonomic ambiguity issues and calculating metrics that describe the structure and diversity of BMI communities. We calculated BMI community metrics with IDAS and calculated the Multimetric Index of Biotic Integrity (MIBI; Klemm et al. 2003, Herlihy et al. 2008) using Microsoft Excel 2010. The MIBI was developed by the US EPA Environmental Monitoring and Assessment Program and was ultimately used for the Wadeable Stream Assessment (US EPA 2006, Herlihy et al. 2008).

The MIBI was developed and regionalized for streams across the contiguous United States. The MIBI used in the ERMN was developed for upland and lowland streams dominated by riffle habitat in the Mid-Atlantic Highlands Region (Klemm et al. 2003). Moreover, the MIBI developed by Klemm et al. (2003) was based on a large dataset of 574 wadeable stream reaches throughout this region and was thoroughly tested.

The MIBI consists of seven metrics selected from 100 metrics that are commonly used for bioassessment and biomonitoring. The metrics chosen were those that performed best in terms of range, precision, responsiveness to various human-induced disturbances, relationship to catchment area, and redundancy (Table 2; Klemm et al. 2003). Most MIBI metrics are counts or proportions of taxa in the community that are characterized as tolerant or intolerant to human perturbations. One of the metrics, the Macroinvertebrate Tolerance Index (MTI), is more complex because it incorporates values (0–10) for each taxon with respect to pollution tolerance (weighted by taxon abundance) and results in higher scores as the proportion of taxa tolerant to general pollution increases (Klemm et al. 2003). Pollution Tolerance Values (PTV) incorporated in the MTI were average tolerances to "various types of stressors" (Klemm et al. 2002).

Table 2. Multimetric Index of Biotic Integrity metric descriptions and their directions of response to increasing human perturbation (Response) from Klemm et al. (2003).

Metric	Description	Response
Ephemeroptera richness	Number of Ephemeroptera (mayfly) taxa	Decrease
Plecoptera richness	Number of Plecoptera (stonefly) taxa	Decrease
Trichoptera richness	Number of Trichoptera (caddisfly) taxa	Decrease
Collector-filterer richness	Number of taxa with a collecting or filtering-feeding strategy	Decrease
Percent non-insect individuals	Percentage of individuals that are not insects	Increase
Macroinvertebrate Tolerance Index	$\sum_i p_i t_i$, where p_i is the proportion of individuals in taxon i and t_i is the pollution tolerance value (PTV) for general pollution	Increase
Percent five dominant taxa	Percentage of individuals in the five numerically dominant taxa	Increase

A particular advantage of the MIBI is that it allows for comparison of biological condition of ERMN streams to condition of streams outside of parks. We compared ERMN stream reaches to conditions reported in the EPA Wadeable Streams Assessment (WSA; EPA 2006); specifically, we compared ERMN stream reach conditions to percentiles (5th and 25th) of MIBI scores at Wadeable Streams Assessment reference sites for aggregated ecoregions (e.g., the Northern Appalachians). In the WSA, these percentiles were used as thresholds to separate poor/fair (5th percentiles) and fair/good (25th percentiles) stream condition classes (Herlilhy 2008).

ERMN and member park staff previously questioned whether comparing ERMN-collected data with WSA results was a valid approach because of perceived methodological differences (e.g., sampling methods and seasons) between the studies. According to Herlihy et al. (2008), a variety of data sources (e.g., state and federal government agencies, universities) were used to conduct the WSA, specifically to establish what constituted 'reference condition' throughout the contiguous United States. According to Herlihy et al. (2008), there were strong effects of data source (e.g., state agency data) on BMI assemblage composition, but those effects were not observed among data collected using USGS, EPA, and Utah State University methods. Because the WSA data collection methods were similar (or identical for the USGS data sources included in the WSA) to those used by the ERMN, it seems reasonable and informative to compare ERMN and WSA results.

Results and Discussion

Allegheny Portage Railroad NHS and Johnstown Flood NMem

2010 Weather and Field Season Summary

All Allegheny Portage Railroad NHS and Johnstown Flood NMem reaches (Figures 2 and 3) were sampled for BMI on October 11, 2010. Benthic macroinvertebrate sampling went well, although stream levels appeared to be slightly lower than in previous years. During sampling, the Millstone Run reach was surveyed for optimal multiprobe deployment locations—a Hach DSX5 multiprobe was later (April 14, 2011) deployed at that site and will continue logging until October 2011.

According to Knight et al. (2011a), calendar year 2010 was only slightly warmer than average in the Allegheny Portage Railroad NHS and Johnstown Flood NMem region, with maximum temperatures averaging very close to normal; between +0.1 to -0.2 degrees Celsius (°C) from normal. The summer months were particularly warm, which were the 30th warmest since records began in 1895, in part due to a very warm July. Precipitation was slightly above normal in 2010 near Allegheny Portage Railroad NHS and Johnstown Flood NMem with several notable dry spells. There was no widespread drought noted in the Allegheny Highlands during 2010, but abnormally dry conditions did occur during late summer and early autumn.

2008–2010 Water Quality

Core water quality parameters were measured once in 2010 (concurrent with BMI sampling), which resulted in three point-in-time samples since 2008. Physical and chemical characteristics of streamwater can vary markedly, both daily and annually. Although there are limitations to point-in-time characterizations of core water quality parameters, these measures can be helpful when evaluating patterns in biological data; moreover, extreme changes to these parameters can sometimes be detected with point-in-time samples. 'Core' water quality parameters (temperature, pH, dissolved oxygen [DO], and specific conductance) were all within established Pennsylvania regulatory criteria (1 Pa. Code § 93; Figures 4 and 5) but it should be again noted that these data are only three instantaneous measurements throughout three years. Consequently, these results should not be considered definitive in regard to streamwater quality, instead, they are meant to provide a general assessment of water quality among sampled reaches. Future efforts will expand upon this initial effort by increasing sampling frequency and breadth of water quality measures.

Specific conductance, a measure of the ability of a substance to conduct electricity, is typically the most consistent of the core parameters under normal conditions. Because specific conductance is relatively stable under normal conditions, observing drastic changes (often increases) in its measurement can indicate potential perturbations (e.g., pollutant spills). The unnamed tributary to South Fork Little Conemaugh River (UNT to SFLCR) at Johnstown Flood NMem had considerably greater specific conductance (244 ± 5 μS/cm; $\bar{x}$ $\pm$SD) than Allegheny Portage Railroad NHS reaches (Figure 4; Appendix A), which likely was a consequence of historical mining activity near Johnstown Flood NMem. Other core water quality parameters (pH, temperature, DO) had similar averages among Allegheny Portage Railroad NHS and Johnstown Flood NMem reaches (Figures 6 and 7), but because these measures vary daily and are related to each other, the wide ranges of pH, temperature, and DO values were not surprising because sampling date and time were different among years.

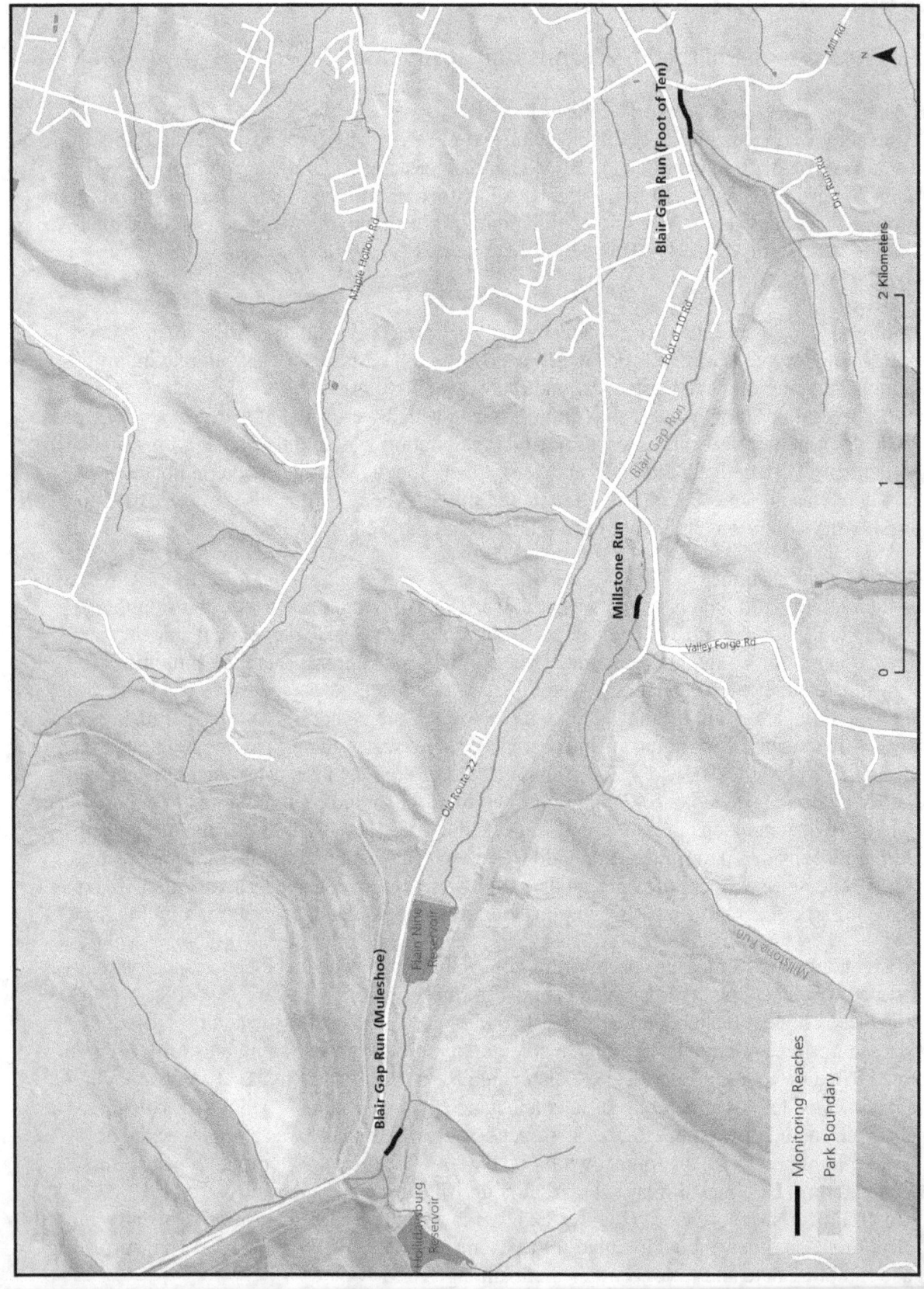

Figure 2. Locations of stream monitoring reaches at Allegheny Portage Railroad National Historic Site.

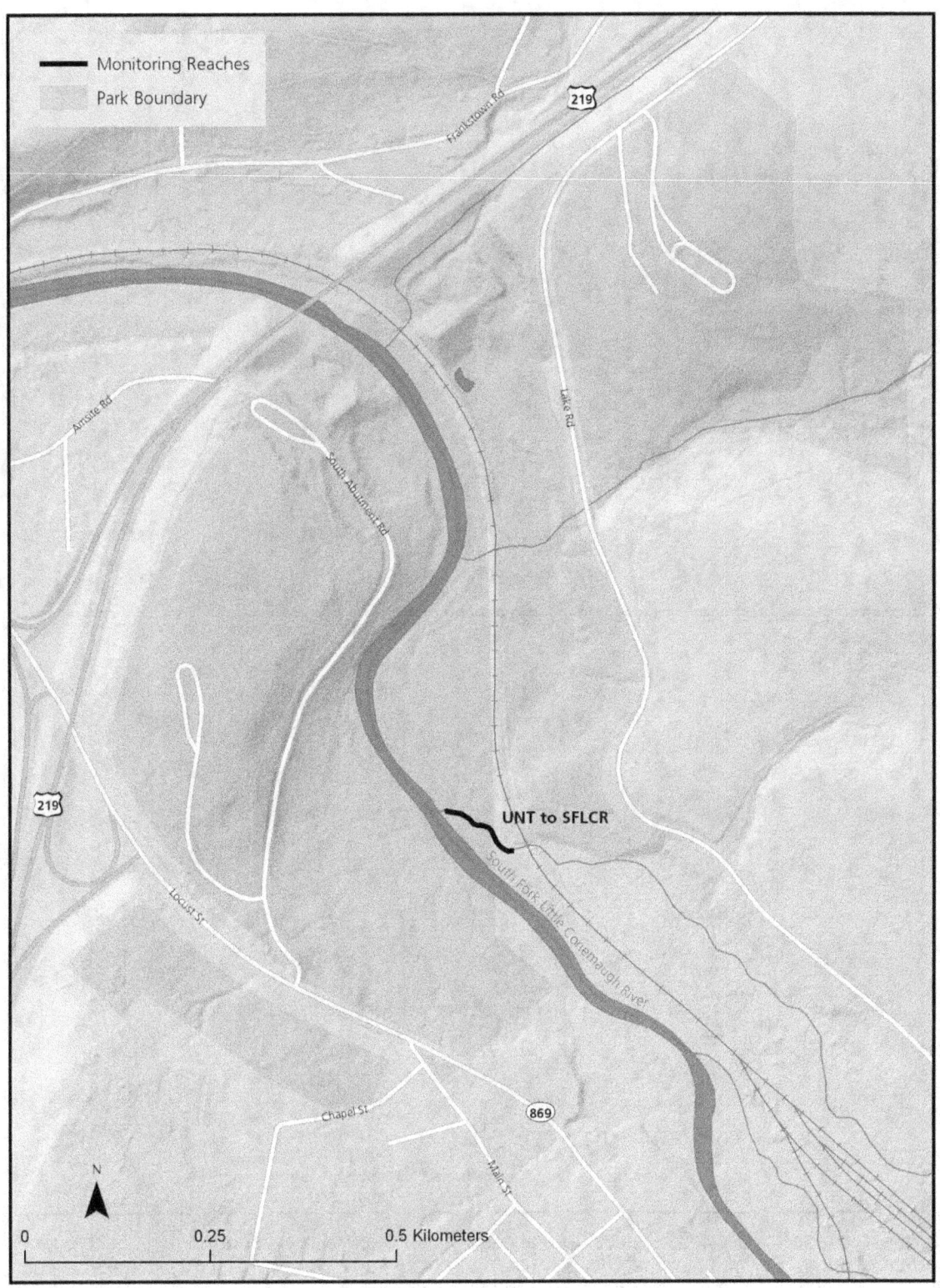

Figure 3. Location of the stream monitoring reach at Johnstown Flood National Memorial.

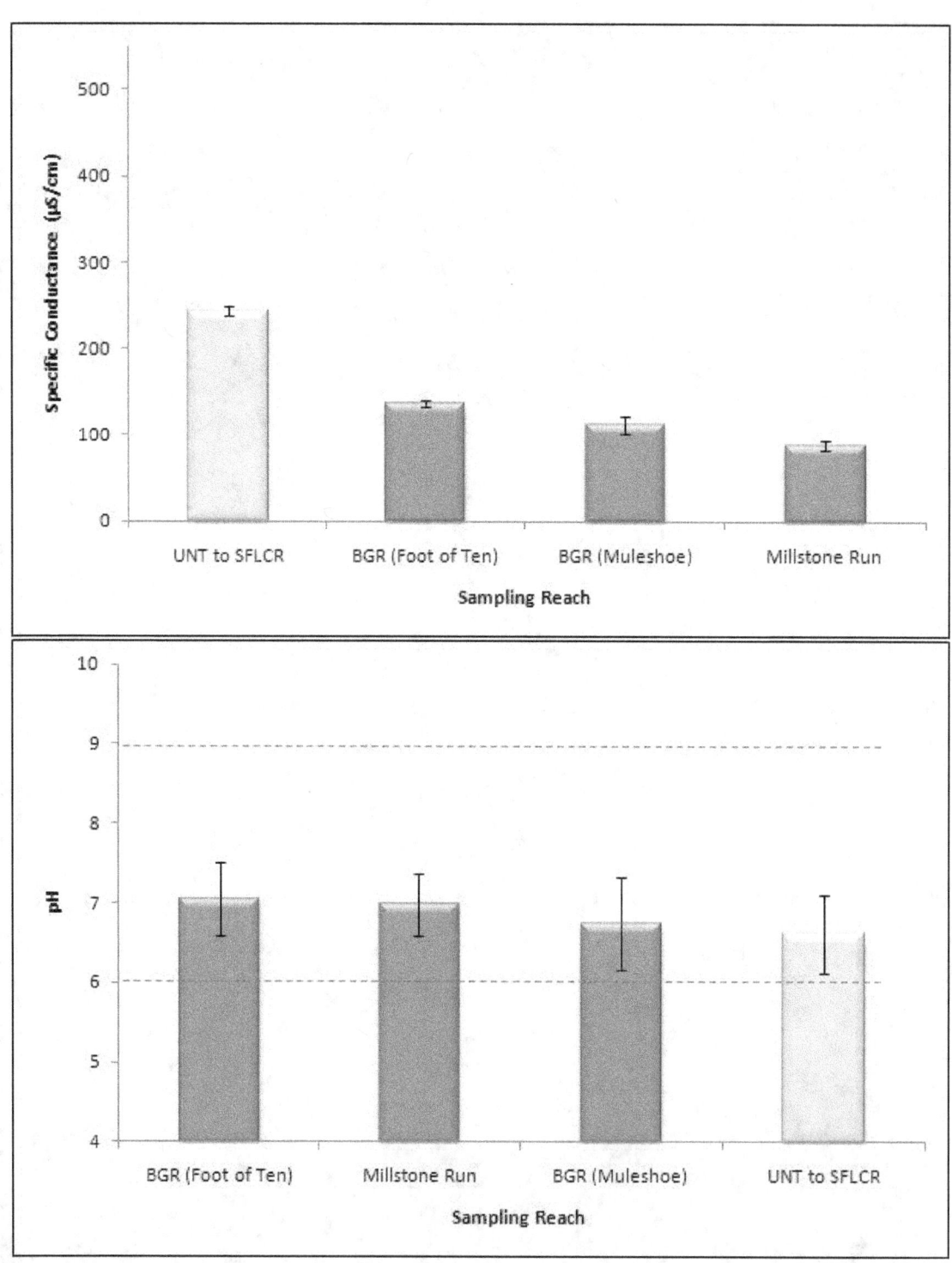

Figure 4. Average specific conductance (top) and pH (bottom) of water at sampling reaches throughout Allegheny Portage Railroad National Historic Site (dark bars) and Johnstown Flood National Memorial (light bar) from 2008–2010 (*n* = 3). Error bars represent one standard deviation whereas dashed lines represent minimum and maximum Pennsylvania regulatory thresholds. BGR = Blair Gap Run; UNT to SFLCR = Unnamed tributary to South Fork Little Conemaugh River.

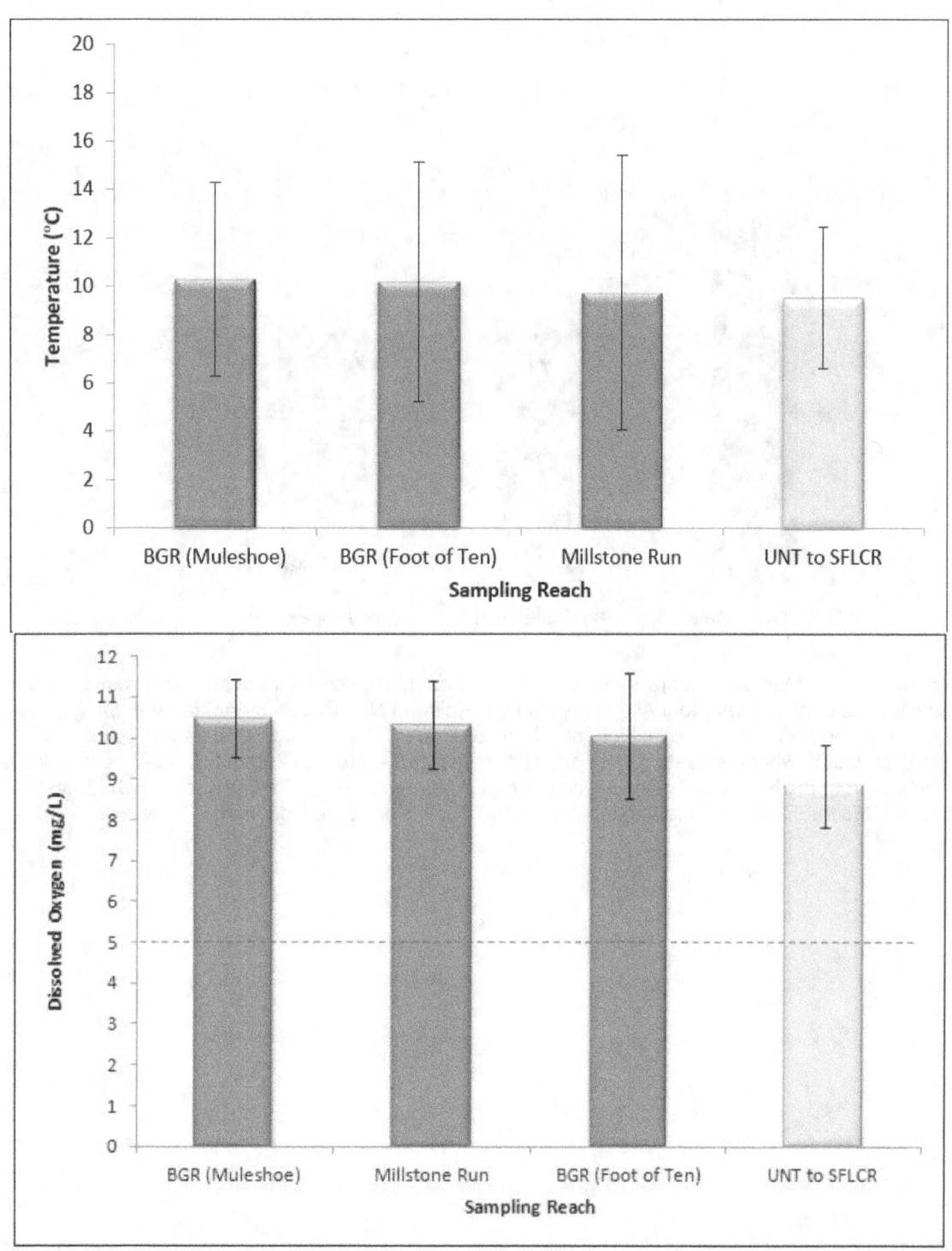

Figure 5. Average temperature (top) and dissolved oxygen concentration (bottom) of water at sampling reaches throughout Allegheny Portage Railroad National Historic Site (dark bars) and Johnstown Flood National Memorial (light bars) from 2008–2010 (*n* = 3). Error bars represent one standard deviation whereas dashed line represents (minimum) Pennsylvania regulatory dissolved oxygen threshold. BGR = Blair Gap Run; UNT to SFLCR = Unnamed tributary to South Fork Little Conemaugh River.

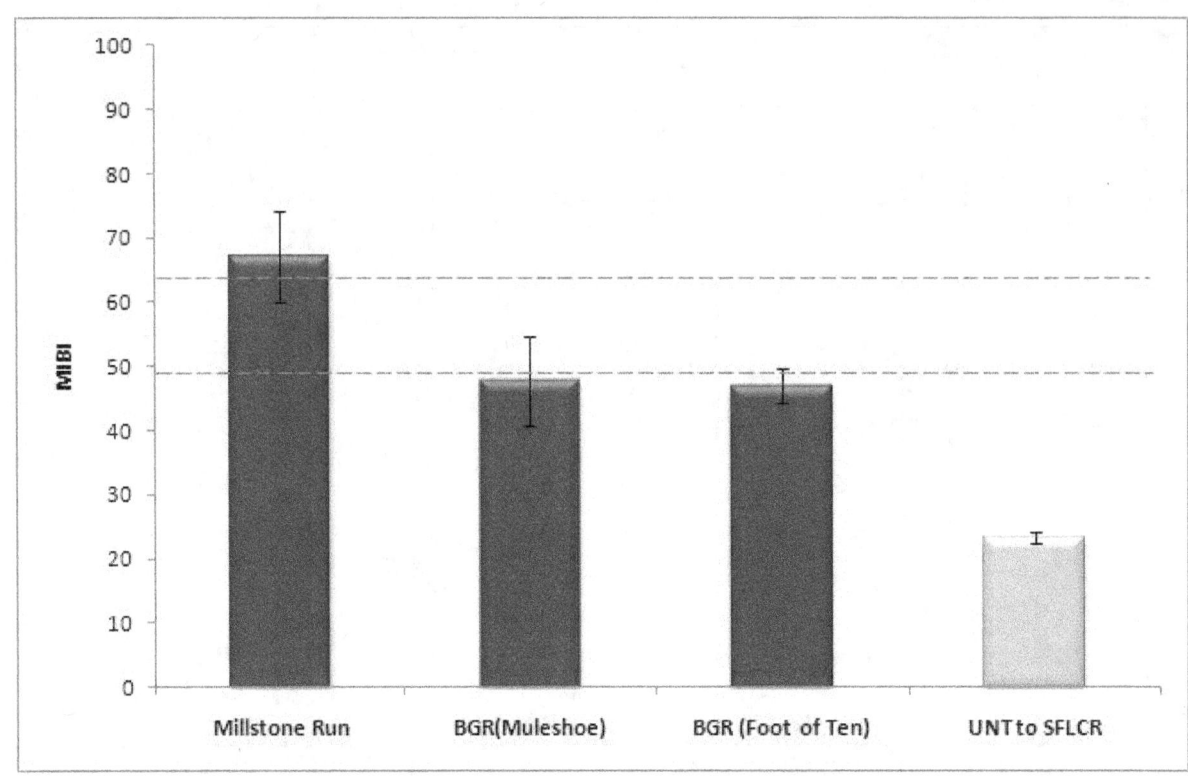

Figure 6. Average Macroinvertebrate Biotic Integrity Index (MIBI) scores for benthic macroinvertebrate assemblages sampled throughout Allegheny Portage Railroad National Historic Site (dark bars) and Johnstown Flood National Memorial (light bar) from 2008 to 2010 (n = 3). Error bars represent one standard deviation, whereas dashed lines depict the 5th (MIBI = 49) and 25th (MIBI = 63) percentiles of MIBI scores from the Northern Appalachians Ecoregion reference sites (Herlihy et al. 2008). BGR = Blair Gap Run; UNT to SFLCR = Unnamed tributary to the South Fork Little Conemaugh River.

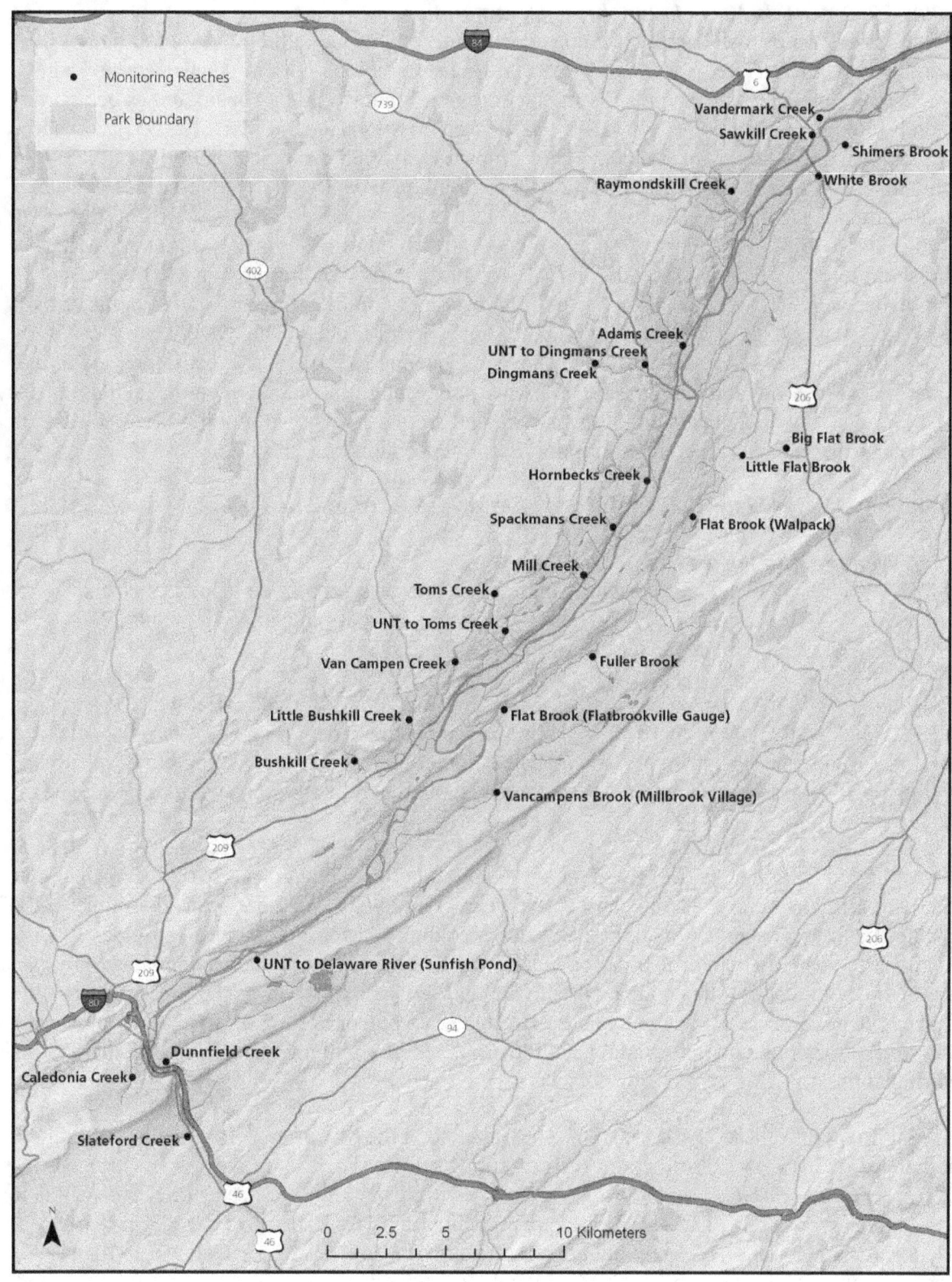

Figure 7. Locations of stream monitoring reaches at Delaware Water Gap National Recreation Area. UNT = Unnamed Tributary.

2008–2010 Benthic Macroinvertebrate Communities

After three years of BMI sampling, a considerable difference in the biological condition of the sampled Allegheny Portage Railroad NHS and Johnstown Flood NMem reaches was evident (Figure 6). The Millstone Run reach was the only reach that would be considered as being in 'good' biological condition (i.e., MIBI $\geq$ 63.0) based on the calculated MIBI (67.05 ± 7.12) and WSA thresholds (Herlihy et al. 2008). The comparatively high ecological integrity of the Millstone Run reach was part of the rationale for long-term deployment of a continuous water quality monitor at that site. The two Blair Gap Run reaches had very similar MIBI scores (Muleshoe = 47.83 ± 6.97; Foot of Ten = 46.96 ± 2.80) which were slightly less than the MIBI threshold for 'fair' biological condition (MIBI = 49.0). Although the average MIBI scores at those sites were in the 'poor' class, variability/uncertainty in the estimate resulted in the error bars (i.e., standard deviation) overlapping the 'fair' condition class. The MIBI score (23.22 ± 0.86) at the UNT to the South Fork Little Conemaugh River was consistently lower than most ERMN reaches and was considered in the 'poor' condition class. Given the land use history (e.g., mining, historical lake bed) of the area in and around Johnstown Flood NMem, it was not surprising that the reach there was in 'poor' biological condition.

Delaware Water Gap NRA and Upper Delaware Scenic SRR

2010 Weather and Field Season Summary

All Delaware Water Gap NRA reaches (Figure 7) were sampled between October 18 and October 25, 2010. As described below, heavy rains throughout fall and early winter 2010 prevented BMI sampling at Upper Delaware SRR (Figure 8) during 2010.

Calendar year 2010 averaged above the long-term mean temperature near Delaware Water Gap NRA and Upper Delaware SRR, with maximum temperatures departing between +0.2 and +1.1°C for the year (Knight et al. 2011b). The summer period was very warm, but despite being in the top 10 warmest summers in 116 years, few daily record maximums were set (Knight et al. 2011b).

According to Knight et al. (2011b), annual precipitation for calendar year 2010 averaged above the long-term mean for the tenth consecutive year. Overall, 2010 had between 84–140 percent of the normal precipitation among regional weather stations. According to a drought index summarized by Knight et al. (2011b), a moist winter reversed into an increasingly dry spring and summer during 2010. When compared with the past few years, 2010 was the first truly dry time during the heart of the growing season (i.e., May to September). However, a historic rainstorm at the start of October completely alleviated the drought and it remained more "moist" than normal during autumn.

Two of the five wettest days during 2010 (as reported at the Matamoras, PA weather station; Knight et al. 2011b) were during the BMI sampling season. The first rain event (mentioned above) occurred on Oct. 1 and totaled 5.05" and delayed sampling for nearly three weeks due to very high stream flows. The second large rain event (1.67") took place on Oct. 27, just after Delaware Water Gap NRA sampling occurred and on the day that Upper Delaware SRR sampling was scheduled to begin. Unfortunately, continued precipitation during November and December maintained elevated stream levels until cold winter temperatures (i.e., below freezing) ultimately prevented samples from being collected at Upper Delaware SRR during 2010.

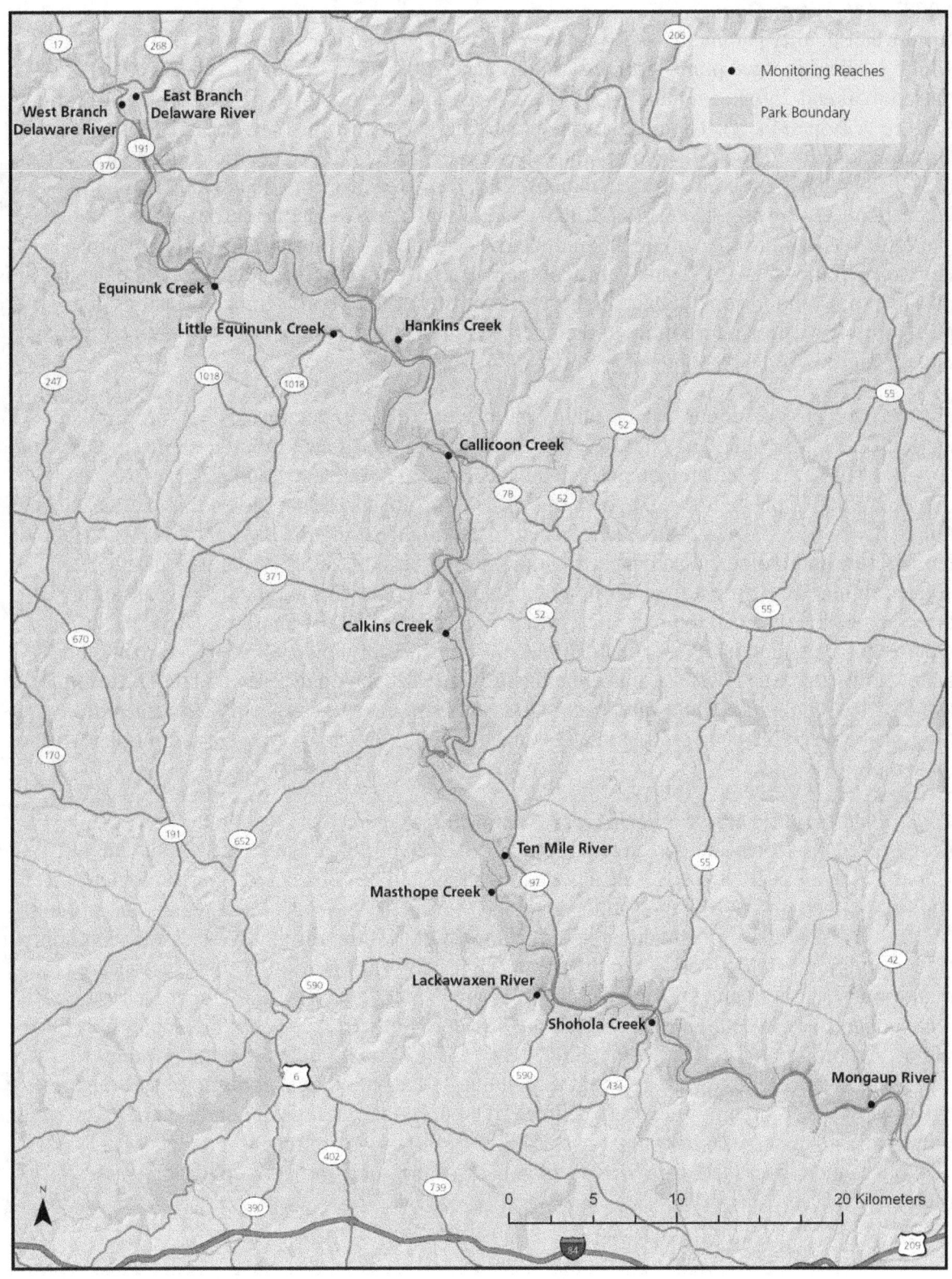

Figure 8. Locations of stream monitoring reaches at Upper Delaware Scenic and Recreational River.

17

2008–2010 Water Quality

Core water quality parameters were measured once in 2010 (concurrent with BMI sampling), which resulted in three point-in-time samples since 2008. Specific conductance was generally between 50 and 250 μs/cm among Delaware Water Gap NRA and Upper Delaware SRR streams (Figure 9; Appendix B). Three Delaware Water Gap NRA streams (Little Flat Brook, Shimers Brook, and White Brook) had comparatively elevated and variable specific conductance values (>300 μs/cm). As ion concentration increases in water, specific conductance increases. Underlying geology of streams is a primary factor that affects ion concentrations and Delaware Water Gap NRA streams with high conductance typically flow through limestone valleys. Human activities (e.g., road salts, effluent) can also raise specific conductance. For example, it is possible that White Brook had the highest (and most variable) conductance measures due, in part, to its downstream proximity to the intersection of several major roads, combined with its underlying limestone geology.

For the most part, other core water quality parameters (pH, temperature, DO) were similar among Delaware Water Gap NRA and Upper Delaware SRR reaches but variable among years (Figures 10–12). These parameters fluctuate daily and are related to each other; consequently, the variability of pH, temperature, and DO values was not surprising, given that there have been only two or three visits to each reach. Generally, sunlight during the day increases water temperature and biological activity, which, in turn, affects measures of pH and DO concentration. Therefore, the time of day that we visited sites among the three years surely affected observed stream temperatures, which in turn, affected pH and DO. The UNT to Delaware River (Sunfish Pond) had pH that was considerably lower (4.95$\pm$0.34) than other Delaware Water Gap NRA streams; whereas, Little Flat Brook generally had the greatest pH (8.55$\pm$0.16). Otherwise, Delaware Water Gap NRA streams were typically circumneutral (i.e., pH between 6.50 and 7.50) and DO concentrations were near or above saturation levels in all sampling reaches.

2008–2010 Benthic Macroinvertebrate Communities

Based on MIBI scores and constituent metrics, 53% (20 of 38) of Delaware Water Gap NRA and Upper Delaware SRR stream reaches were in what would be considered 'fair' biological condition based upon MIBI thresholds developed for the EPA Wadeable Streams Assessment (Figure 13; EPA 2006). It should be noted that most of the streams that were assessed as being in 'fair' condition had MIBI scores in the upper (i.e., MIBI >56) portion of that class; nearer 'good' than 'poor.' Furthermore, streams within Delaware Water Gap NRA and Upper Delaware SRR were collectively in better condition than the broader Northern Appalachians Ecoregion (EPA 2006). According to the WSA (EPA 2006), only 13% of stream miles in the Northern Appalachians Ecoregion were assessed as being in 'good' biological condition based on the MIBI and 45% of stream miles were deemed to be in 'poor' ecological condition (27% of stream miles were not assessed). In comparison, 24% (9 of 38) of stream reaches in Delaware Water Gap NRA and Upper Delaware SRR were in each of the good and poor condition classes, respectively.

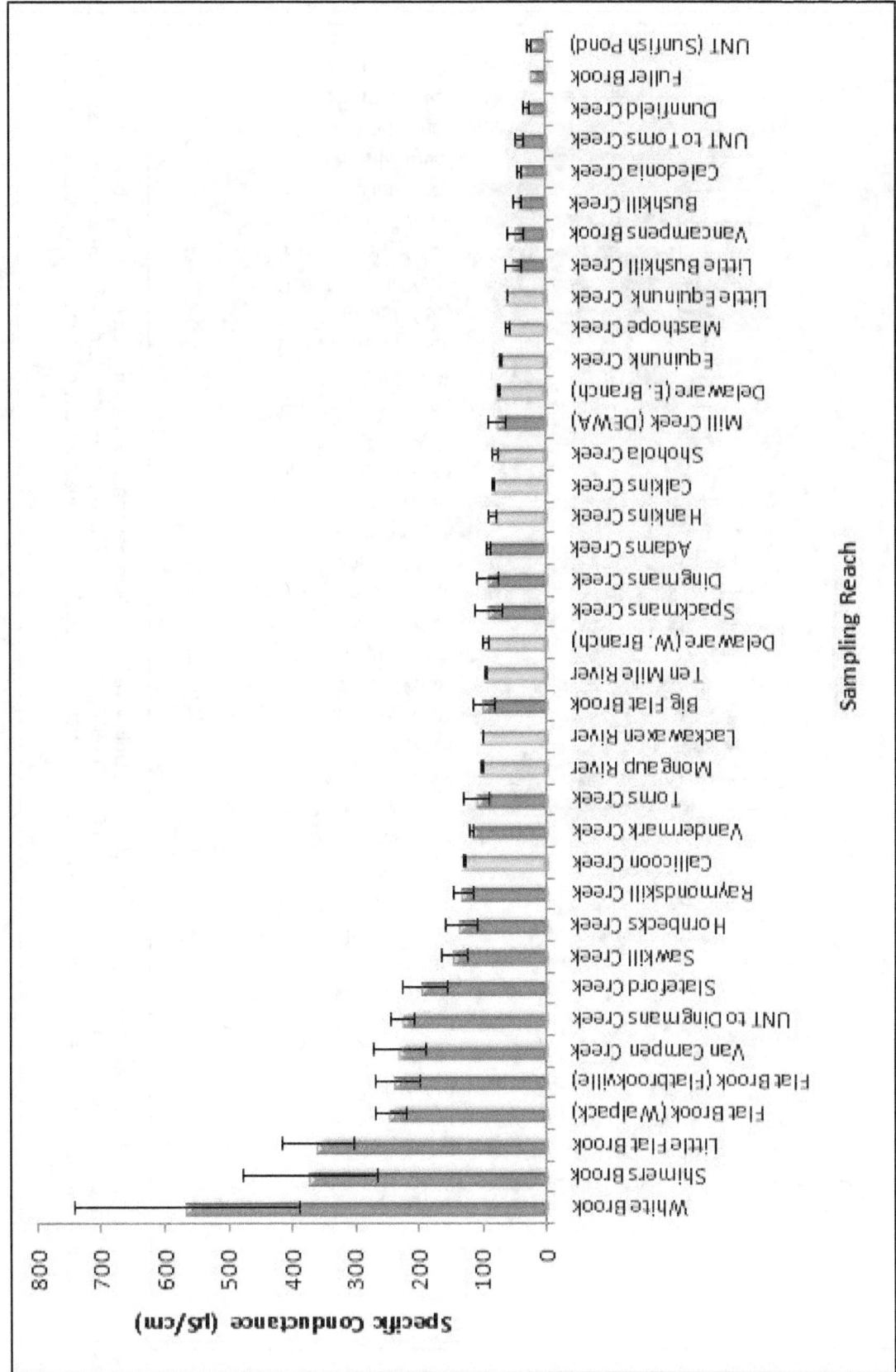

Figure 9. Average specific conductance of water at sampling reaches throughout Delaware Water Gap National Recreation Area (*n* = 3; dark bars) and Upper Delaware Scenic and Recreational River (*n* = 2; light bars) from 2008–2010. Error bars represent one standard deviation.

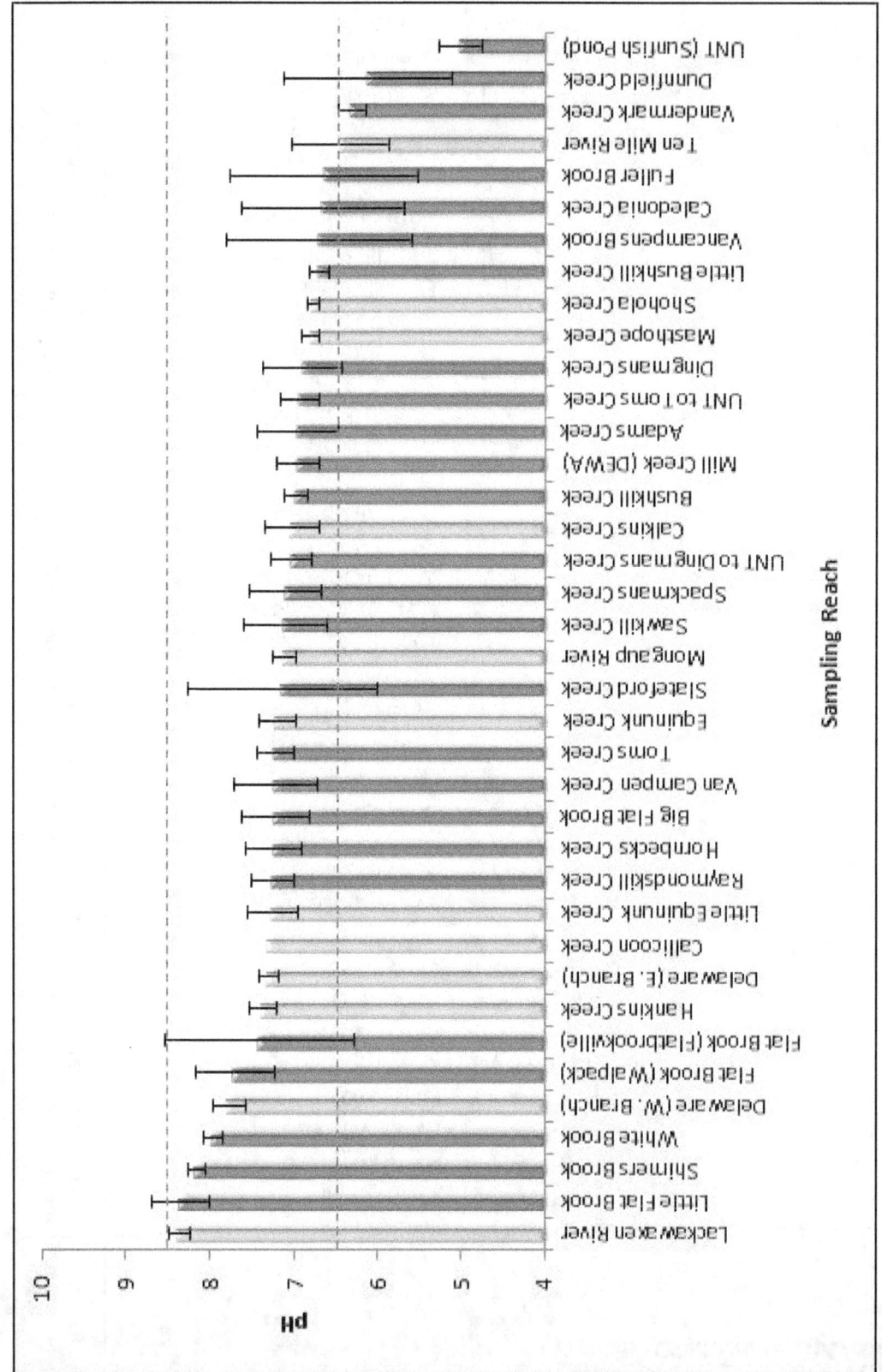

Figure 10. Average pH of water at sampling reaches throughout Delaware Water Gap National Recreation Area (n = 3; dark bars) and Upper Delaware Scenic and Recreational River (n = 2; light bars) from 2008–2010. Error bars represent one standard deviation whereas dashed lines are provided as reference to represent the minimum and maximum New York regulatory criteria, which are the most stringent criteria among Pennsylvania, New Jersey, and New York.

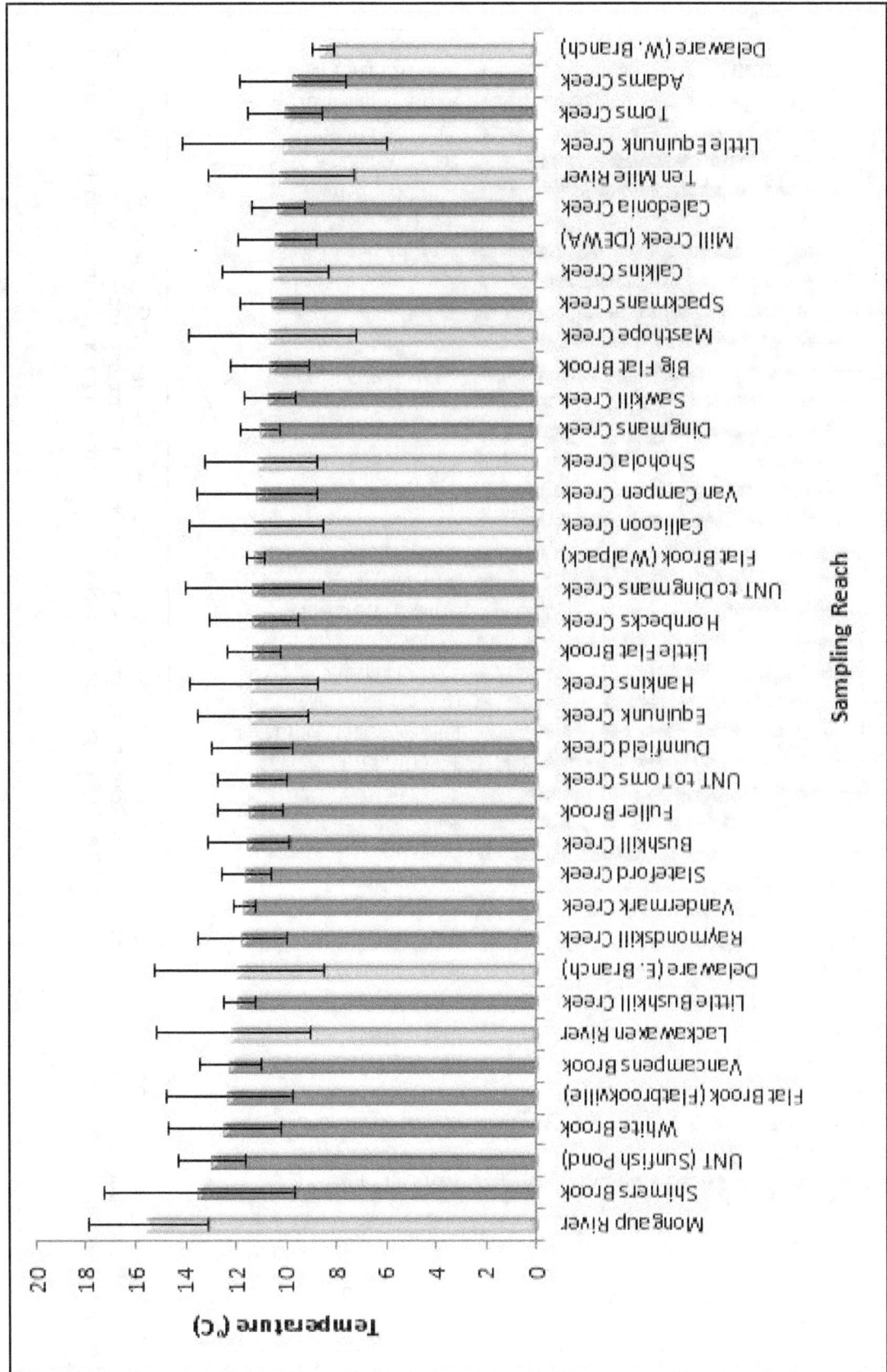

Figure 11. Average water temperature at sampling reaches throughout Delaware Water Gap National Recreation Area (*n* = 3; dark bars) and Upper Delaware Scenic and Recreational River (*n* = 2; light bars) from 2008–2010. Error bars represent one standard deviation.

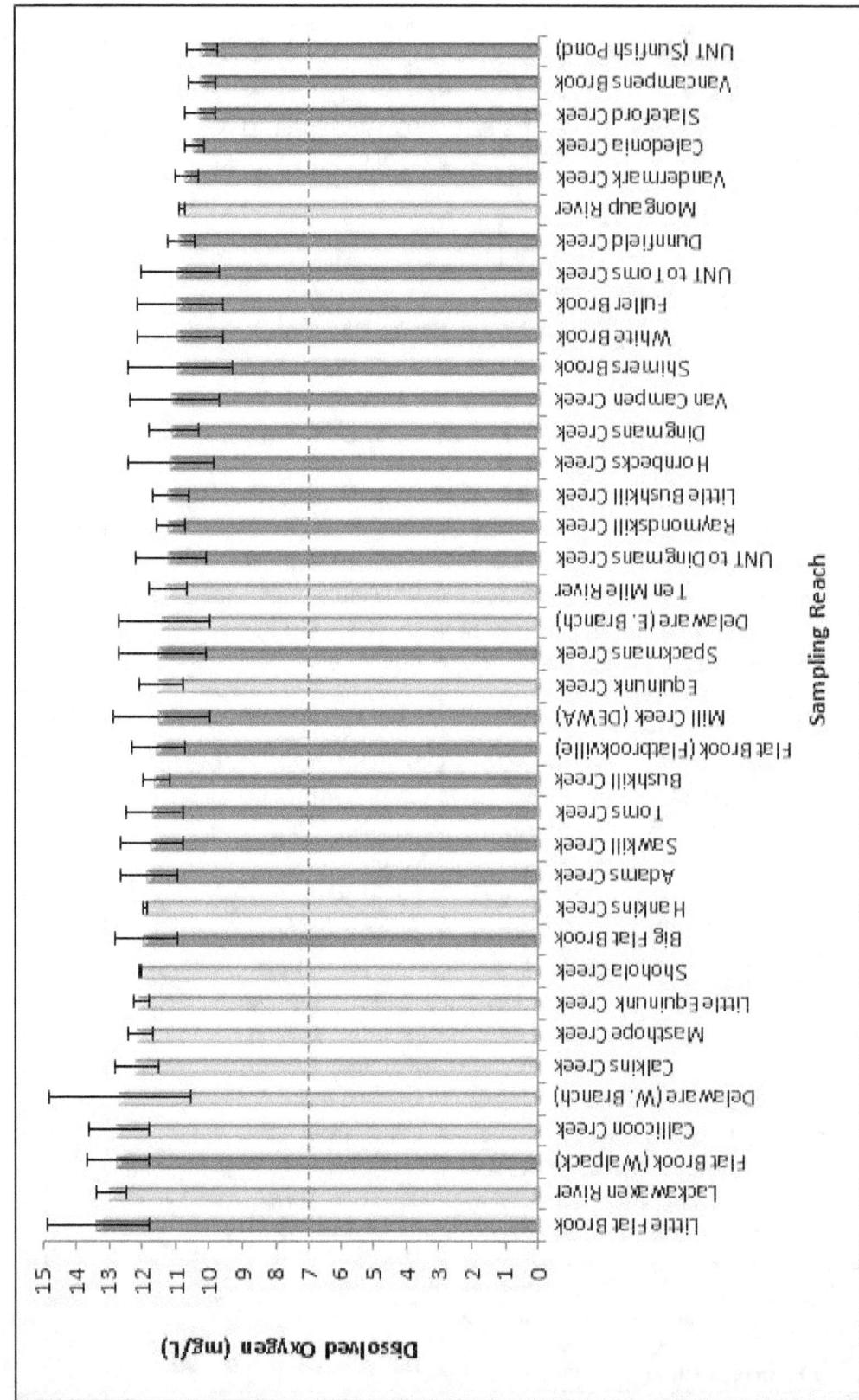

Figure 12. Average dissolved oxygen concentration of water at sampling reaches throughout Delaware Water Gap National Recreation Area (*n* = 3; dark bars) and Upper Delaware Scenic and Recreational River (*n* = 2; light bars) from 2008–2010. Error bars represent one standard deviation whereas the dashed line represents the most stringent (i.e., highest) minimum dissolved oxygen criterion among Pennsylvania, New Jersey, and New York.

22

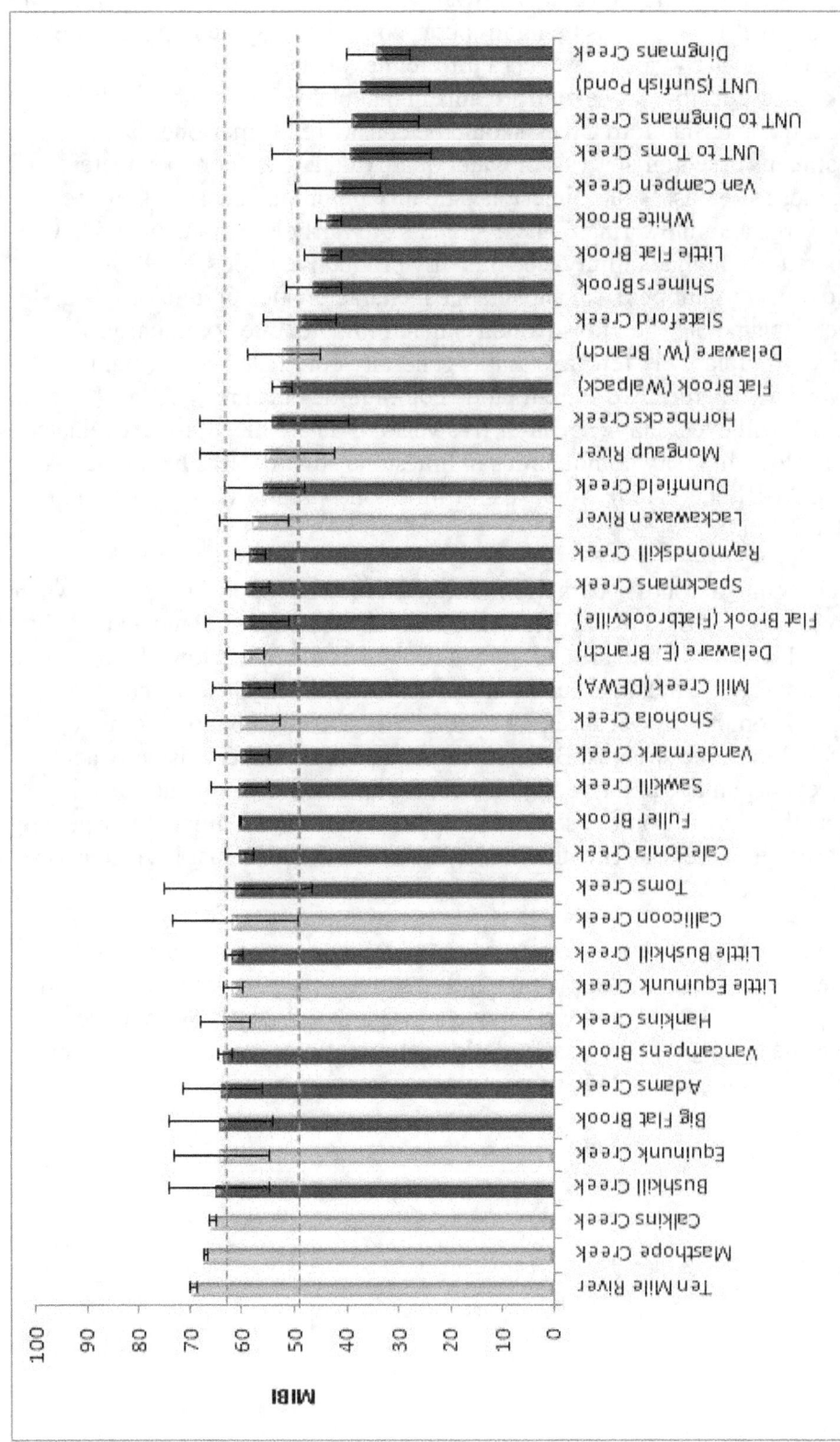

Figure 13. Average Macroinvertebrate Biotic Integrity Index (MIBI) scores for benthic macroinvertebrate samples collected throughout Delaware Water Gap National Recreation Area (*n* = 3; dark bars) and Upper Delaware Scenic and Recreational River (*n* = 2; light bars) from 2008–2010. Error bars represent one standard deviation, whereas dashed lines depict the 5th (MIBI = 49) and 25th (MIBI = 63) percentiles of MIBI scores from the Northern Appalachians Ecoregion reference sites (Herlihy et al. 2008).

Although no Upper Delaware SRR streams were assessed in the 'poor' condition class, nine Delaware Water Gap NRA streams were. Several Delaware Water Gap NRA streams (e.g., Van Campen Creek, Dingmans Creek) assessed as being in 'poor' condition may be impaired due to historical and/or ongoing human activities; however, a different explanation for that classification is more likely responsible for several streams in that class. Little Flat Brook, Shimers Brook, White Brook, and Slateford Creek should be considered 'limestone' or 'limestone-influenced' streams based on analysis of water quality data (e.g., core parameters) and geology underlying those streams. 'True' limestone streams are unique because they are formed or maintained by large alkaline springs. These streams are fairly low gradient and have relatively constant temperatures, high alkalinity, and are very productive (Botts 2009); consequently, their relatively constant physical and chemical characteristics produce a distinctive, abundant, yet depauperate (i.e., low diversity) macroinvertebrate community. The end result is a community with relatively few taxa that is generally dominated by several taxa. Because limestone streams yield naturally different biotic communities than most ERMN streams, those communities will eventually (i.e., after five years of data collection) be evaluated with an index designed for low-diversity communities in limestone streams. It is likely that we will use, in addition to the MIBI, the PA DEP indexes for limestone streams (Botts 2009) and freestone streams (PA DEP 2009).

A freestone stream (UNT [Sunfish Pond]) poses a similar, but somewhat opposite problem when estimating biological condition based on the MIBI. That stream drains Sunfish Pond and nearby wetlands on the Kittatinny Ridge, which in all likelihood accounts for the very low pH (5.0+0.3) observed there. In bog habitats (e.g., in and around Sunfish Pond), naturally low pH conditions result in a depauperate BMI community because of a similar but opposite (i.e., low vs. high pH) phenomenon that occurs in limestone streams. Because bog outflows have a consistently acidic character, the relatively few taxa that can thrive in those conditions tend to dominate. Despite having relatively few taxa that may in some cases be indicative of abandoned mine drainage, bog outflows are not necessarily 'impaired' — it is their natural, acidic condition that leads to a low MIBI score.

There was obvious variability in MIBI scores among years, which was not surprising based on environmental differences. For example, precipitation and stream levels were lower than normal during fall 2008, near typical in fall 2009, and well above average in fall 2010. Not only do environmental differences have the potential to affect BMI community composition, they can also affect sampling efficiency and associated error.

Literature Cited

Barbour, M. T., J. Gerritsen, B. D. Snyder, and J. B. Stribling. 1999. Rapid bioassessment protocols for use in streams and wadeable rivers: periphyton, benthic macroinvertebrates and fish, second edition. EPA 841-B-99-002. U.S. Environmental Protection Agency. Office of Water. Washington, DC.

Botts, W. 2009. An index of biological integrity (IBI) for "true" limestone streams. Pennsylvania Department of Environmental Protection. Harrisburg, PA. 39 pp.

Carter, J. L., and V. H. Resh. 2001. After site selection and before data analysis: sampling, sorting, and laboratory procedures used in stream benthic macroinvertebrate monitoring programs by USA state agencies. Journal of the North American Benthological Society 20(4):658–682.

Delaware River Basin Commission (DRBC). 2010. 2010 Delaware River and Bay Integrated List Water Quality Assessment. Trenton, NJ. Accessed Sept. 27 2011. http://www/.state.nj.us/drbc/10IntegratedList/FinalReport.pdf.

Fancy, S. G., J. E. Gross, and S. L. Carter. 2009. Monitoring the condition of natural resources in US national parks. Environmental Monitoring and Assessment 151:161–174.

Herlihy, A. T., S. G. Paulsen, J. Van Sickle, J. L. Stoddard, C. P. Hawkins, and L. L. Yuan. 2008. Striving for consistency in a national assessment: the challenges of applying a reference-condition approach at a continental scale. Journal of the North American Benthological Society 27(4):860–877.

Klemm, D. J., K. A. Blocksom, W. T. Thoeny, F. A. Fulk, A. T. Herlihy, P. R. Kaufmann, and S. M. Cormier. 2002. Methods development and use of macroinvertebrates as indicators of ecological conditions for streams in the mid-Atlantic highlands region. Environmental Monitoring and Assessment 78:169–212.

Klemm, D. J., K. A. Blocksom, F. A. Fulk, A. T. Herlihy, R. M. Hughes, P. R. Kaufmann, D. V.Peck, J. L. Stoddard, W. T. Thoeny, M. B. Griffith, and W. S. Davis. 2003. Development and evaluation of a macroinvertebrate biotic integrity index (MBII) for regionally assessing mid-Atlantic highlands streams. Environmental Management 31(5):656–669.

Knight, P., T. Wisniewski, C. Bahrmann, and S. Miller. 2011a. Weather of Allegheny Portage Railroad National Historic Site and Johnstown Flood National Memorial: Eastern Rivers and Mountains Network summary report for 2010. Natural Resource Data Series NPS/ERMN/NRDS—2011/290. National Park Service, Fort Collins, CO.

Knight, P., T. Wisniewski, C. Bahrmann, and S. Miller. 2011b. Weather of Delaware Water Gap National Recreation Area and Upper Delaware Scenic and Recreational River: Eastern Rivers and Mountains Network summary report for 2010. Natural Resource Data Series NPS/ERMN/NRDS—2011/292. National Park Service, Fort Collins, CO.

Marshall, M. R., and N. B. Piekielek. 2007. Eastern Rivers and Mountains Network ecological monitoring plan. Natural Resource Report NPS/ERMN/NRR—2007/017. National Park Service, Fort Collins, CO.

Mattsson, B. J., and M. R. Marshall. 2009. Streamside bird monitoring protocol for the Eastern Rivers and Mountains Network. Technical Report NPS/ERMN/NRR—2009/DRAFT. National Park Service, Fort Collins, CO.

Moulton, S. R., J. L. Carter, S. A. Grotheer, T. F. Cuffney, and T. M. Short. 2000. Methods of analysis by the U.S. Geological Survey National Water Quality Laboratory—processing, taxonomy, and quality control of benthic macroinvertebrate samples. U.S. Geological Society Open-File Report 00-212. 61 pp.

Moulton, S. R., J. G. Kennen, R. M. Goldstein, and J. A. Hambrook. 2002. Revised protocols for sampling algal, invertebrate and fish communities as part of the National Water-Quality Assessment Program: U.S. Geological Survey Open-File Report 02-150. 87 pp.

National Park Service (NPS). 1999. Natural resource challenge: the National Park Service's action plan for preserving natural resources. US Department of the Interior, National Park Service. Washington, DC. http://www.nature.nps.gov/challenge/challengedoc/index.htm. Accessed 10/6/10.

National Park Service (NPS). 2008. Guidance for designing an integrated monitoring program. http://science.nature.nps.gov/im/monitor/GoalsObjectives.cfm#Integration. Accessed February 4, 2008.

Pennsylvania Department of Environmental Protection (PA DEP). 2009. A benthic index of biotic integrity for wadeable freestone riffle-run streams in Pennsylvania (draft). Harrisburg, PA. 122 pp.

Perles, S. J., J. C. Finley, and M. R. Marshall. 2009. Vegetation and soil monitoring protocol for the Eastern Rivers and Mountains Network. Natural Resource Report NPS/ERMN/NRR—2009/DRAFT. National Park Service, Fort Collins, CO.

Tzilkowski, C. J., A. S. Weber, and C. P. Ferreri. 2009. Benthic macroinvertebrate monitoring protocol for wadeable streams in the Eastern Rivers and Mountains Network. Natural Resource Report NPS/ERMN/NRR—2009/DRAFT. National Park Service, Fort Collins, CO.

United States Environmental Protection Agency (US EPA). 2006. Wadeable streams assessment: a collaborative survey of the Nation's streams. EPA841-B-06-002. Washington, DC.

Appendix A. Core water quality parameter measurements throughout Eastern Rivers and Mountains Network wadeable streams during 2008–2010 field seasons.

Park[1]	Reach Name	n	Temp[2]	SD[3]	pH	SD	DO[4]	SD	SpC[5]	SD
ALPO	Blair Gap Run (Foot of Ten)	3	10.2	4.9	7.1	0.5	10.1	1.5	137.2	4.0
ALPO	Blair Gap Run (Muleshoe)	3	10.3	4.0	6.7	0.6	10.5	0.9	112.6	10.1
ALPO	Millstone Run	3	9.7	5.7	7.0	0.4	10.3	1.1	88.7	5.5
DEWA	Adams Creek	3	9.7	2.1	7.0	0.5	11.8	0.9	91.9	2.8
DEWA	Big Flat Brook	3	10.6	1.6	7.2	0.4	11.9	0.9	99.2	17.3
DEWA	Bushkill Creek	3	11.5	1.6	7.0	0.1	11.6	0.4	44.8	5.8
DEWA	Caledonia Creek	3	10.3	1.1	6.7	1.0	10.5	0.3	42.1	3.4
DEWA	Dingmans Creek	3	11.0	0.8	6.9	0.5	11.1	0.7	92.0	16.5
DEWA	Dunnfield Creek	3	11.4	1.6	6.1	1.0	10.9	0.4	30.5	4.3
DEWA	Flat Brook (Flatbrookville)	2	12.3	2.5	7.4	1.1	11.5	0.8	234.5	36.1
DEWA	Flat Brook (Walpack)	2	11.2	0.4	7.7	0.5	12.7	0.9	246.0	24.0
DEWA	Fuller Brook	2	11.5	1.3	6.6	1.1	10.9	1.3	27.0	*
DEWA	Hornbecks Creek	3	11.3	1.8	7.3	0.3	11.2	1.3	133.2	24.7
DEWA	Little Bushkill Creek	3	11.9	0.6	6.7	0.1	11.2	0.5	52.1	13.3
DEWA	Little Flat Brook	3	11.3	1.1	8.4	0.3	13.3	1.5	359.8	56.8
DEWA	Mill Creek	3	10.3	1.6	7.0	0.3	11.5	1.4	76.6	13.9
DEWA	Raymondskill Creek	3	11.8	1.7	7.3	0.2	11.2	0.5	132.4	15.0
DEWA	Sawkill Creek	3	10.6	1.0	7.1	0.5	11.7	0.9	144.8	19.3
DEWA	Shimers Brook	3	13.5	3.8	8.2	0.1	10.9	1.6	372.1	106.5
DEWA	Slateford Creek	3	11.6	1.0	7.1	1.1	10.3	0.5	191.5	35.6
DEWA	Spackmans Creek	3	10.5	1.3	7.1	0.4	11.4	1.3	92.8	21.2
DEWA	Toms Creek	3	10.0	1.5	7.2	0.2	11.7	0.9	110.8	20.0
DEWA	UNT (Sunfish Pond)	3	13.0	1.4	5.0	0.3	10.2	0.5	26.7	2.5
DEWA	UNT to Dingmans Creek	3	11.3	2.7	7.0	0.2	11.2	1.0	226.5	19.0
DEWA	UNT to Toms Creek	3	11.4	1.4	6.9	0.2	10.9	1.1	42.1	5.9
DEWA	Van Campen Creek	3	11.1	2.4	7.2	0.5	11.1	1.3	231.5	40.8
DEWA	Vancampens Brook	3	12.2	1.2	6.7	1.1	10.2	0.4	49.1	12.1
DEWA	Vandermark Creek	3	11.7	0.4	6.3	0.2	10.7	0.4	119.0	2.6
DEWA	White Brook	3	12.4	2.2	8.0	0.1	10.9	1.3	565.3	176.4
JOFL	UNT to SFLCR	3	9.5	2.9	6.6	0.5	8.8	1.0	243.8	4.8
UPDE	Calkins Creek	2	10.4	2.1	7.0	0.3	12.2	0.7	83.9	0.1
UPDE	Callicoon Creek	2	11.2	2.7	7.3	*	12.7	0.9	130.3	2.5
UPDE	Delaware (East Branch)	2	11.9	3.4	7.3	0.1	11.4	1.3	74.8	1.8
UPDE	Delaware (West Branch)	2	8.5	0.4	7.8	0.2	12.7	2.1	95.5	4.9
UPDE	Equinunk Creek	2	11.3	2.2	7.2	0.2	11.5	0.7	71.8	1.1
UPDE	Hankins Creek	2	11.3	2.5	7.4	0.2	11.9	0.1	84.6	6.4
UPDE	Lackawaxen River	2	12.1	3.1	8.4	0.1	13.0	0.4	102.1	0.1
UPDE	Little Equinunk Creek	2	10.0	4.1	7.3	0.3	12.1	0.2	60.5	0.7
UPDE	Masthope Creek	2	10.5	3.3	6.8	0.1	12.1	0.4	61.9	2.6
UPDE	Mongaup River	2	15.5	2.4	7.1	0.1	10.8	0.1	103.3	1.8
UPDE	Shohola Creek	2	11.0	2.2	6.8	0.1	12.1	0.0	80.6	3.5
UPDE	Ten Mile River	2	10.2	2.9	6.5	0.6	11.2	0.6	96.1	1.5

---

[1] ALPO = Allegheny Portage Railroad National Historic Site, DEWA = Delaware Water Gap National Recreation Area, JOFL = Johnstown Flood National Memorial, UPDE = Upper Delaware Scenic and Recreational River
[2] Water temperature
[3] Standard deviation
[4] Dissolved oxygen
[5] Specific conductance

Appendix B. Benthic macroinvertebrate community metrics and indices from wadeable streams throughout national parks in the northern Appalachians ecoregion of the Eastern Rivers and Mountains Network (2008–2010). All metrics and indices presented are expected to respond positively with increasing ecological integrity, except for two metrics (%Non-insect and %5dominant) and the Macroinvertebrate Tolerance Index (MTI) which are expected to respond positively. See footnotes for metric and index descriptions.

Park[1]	Stream	Date	Taxa[2]	EPT[3]	E[4]	P[5]	T[6]	C-F[7]	%Non-insect[8]	%5 dominant[9]	MTI[10]	MIBI[11]
ALPO	Millstone Run	10/31/2008	31	20	9	6	5	4	1.88	53.69	3.23	59.79
ALPO	Millstone Run	10/21/2009	42	23	7	8	8	4	0.52	54.38	3.25	67.34
ALPO	Millstone Run	10/11/2010	40	25	11	6	8	5	1.21	43.51	3.51	74.01
ALPO	Blair Gap Run (Muleshoe)	10/31/2008	25	18	7	4	7	6	28.44	59.38	4.41	39.91
ALPO	Blair Gap Run (Muleshoe)	10/21/2009	31	20	7	5	8	6	12.34	56.17	4.10	50.57
ALPO	Blair Gap Run (Muleshoe)	10/11/2010	28	17	5	5	7	6	5.11	67.41	3.63	53.00
ALPO	Blair Gap Run (Foot of Ten)	10/31/2008	28	15	5	3	7	7	10.90	62.70	4.23	44.06
ALPO	Blair Gap Run (Foot of Ten)	10/21/2009	29	15	4	2	9	8	5.45	74.28	3.97	47.19
ALPO	Blair Gap Run (Foot of Ten)	10/11/2010	26	17	6	3	8	7	1.79	81.50	3.80	49.65
DEWA	White Brook	10/1/2008	22	11	2	3	6	4	1.41	65.19	3.51	45.32
DEWA	White Brook	10/1/2009	27	14	3	4	7	4	0.73	78.45	3.47	44.31
DEWA	White Brook	10/18/2010	23	13	3	4	6	3	1.13	83.93	3.15	40.63
DEWA	Dunnfield Creek	10/2/2008	37	22	8	6	8	3	3.79	54.14	3.80	59.90
DEWA	Dunnfield Creek	10/2/2009	29	22	7	6	9	3	2.92	53.90	3.68	60.22
DEWA	Dunnfield Creek	10/19/2010	31	19	6	5	8	3	7.72	69.05	3.55	47.09
DEWA	UNT to Delaware River (Sunfish Pond)	10/2/2008	21	13	1	6	6	3	5.00	67.69	3.63	47.15
DEWA	UNT to Delaware River (Sunfish Pond)	10/7/2009	23	13	0	4	9	2	2.97	73.30	4.06	40.79
DEWA	UNT to Delaware River (Sunfish Pond)	10/19/2010	16	9	0	3	6	4	12.68	83.10	4.59	22.71

[1] ALPO = Allegheny Portage Railroad National Historic Site, DEWA = Delaware Water Gap National Recreation Area, JOFL = Johnstown Flood National Memorial, UPDE = Upper Delaware Scenic and Recreational River
[2] Total distinct taxa
[3] Taxa in the insect orders Ephemeroptera, Plecoptera, and Trichoptera
[4] Ephemeroptera taxa
[5] Plecoptera taxa
[6] Trichoptera taxa
[7] Taxa in the 'collector' or 'filterer' functional feeding groups
[8] Percentage of non-insect individuals in the assemblage
[9] Percentage of individuals comprised by the five dominant taxa
[10] Macroinvertebrate Tolerance Index
[11] Multimetric Index of Biological Integrity

Park[1]	Stream	Date	Taxa[2]	EPT[3]	E[4]	P[5]	T[6]	C-F[7]	%Non-insect[8]	%5 dominant[9]	MTI[10]	MIBI[11]
DEWA	Vancampens Brook (Millbrook Village)	10/2/2008	35	24	8	5	11	4	0.36	51.93	3.53	62.57
DEWA	Vancampens Brook (Millbrook Village)	10/7/2009	33	24	9	6	9	4	1.80	52.54	3.48	65.06
DEWA	Vancampens Brook (Millbrook Village)	10/19/2010	36	25	9	5	11	5	0.68	60.15	3.33	62.86
DEWA	Slateford Creek	10/3/2008	28	13	3	4	6	4	9.16	63.00	3.39	41.02
DEWA	Slateford Creek	10/2/2009	30	19	5	5	9	3	2.17	58.70	3.21	53.98
DEWA	Slateford Creek	10/19/2010	29	17	5	6	6	2	5.28	57.76	3.56	51.89
DEWA	Caledonia Creek	10/3/2008	38	22	8	7	7	4	2.42	58.50	3.37	63.28
DEWA	Caledonia Creek	10/2/2009	31	20	6	6	8	3	0.34	62.29	3.40	57.95
DEWA	Caledonia Creek	10/19/2010	31	23	7	6	10	3	0.00	60.34	3.43	60.40
DEWA	Fuller Brook	10/3/2008	30	19	4	7	8	3	0.13	55.27	3.56	60.53
DEWA	Fuller Brook	10/19/2010	35	20	6	6	8	3	1.00	54.21	3.62	60.47
DEWA	Van Campen Creek	10/5/2008	32	18	5	4	9	5	14.04	61.84	4.17	39.00
DEWA	Van Campen Creek	10/9/2009	35	22	7	4	11	5	5.59	59.17	4.01	51.01
DEWA	Van Campen Creek	10/20/2010	32	18	5	3	10	7	22.11	69.43	4.31	35.23
DEWA	Little Bushkill Creek	10/5/2008	39	23	9	3	11	8	10.22	48.83	3.64	62.62
DEWA	Little Bushkill Creek	10/8/2009	40	25	10	5	10	4	7.52	52.04	3.58	59.69
DEWA	Little Bushkill Creek	10/25/2010	39	25	7	5	13	8	5.55	59.62	3.53	62.88
DEWA	UNT to Dingmans Creek	10/5/2008	25	9	1	2	6	6	34.36	64.72	4.91	26.18
DEWA	UNT to Dingmans Creek	10/6/2009	32	20	6	5	9	8	15.46	52.56	4.27	51.03
DEWA	UNT to Dingmans Creek	10/20/2010	38	21	5	4	12	6	18.19	58.34	4.26	38.74
DEWA	Toms Creek	10/7/2008	32	20	7	5	8	5	20.50	51.87	4.16	45.09
DEWA	Toms Creek	10/8/2009	33	25	8	6	11	5	7.50	41.56	3.65	65.06
DEWA	Toms Creek	10/20/2010	44	29	11	7	11	6	6.66	47.67	3.66	72.64
DEWA	UNT to Toms Creek	10/6/2008	29	19	8	3	8	5	6.11	71.55	4.51	42.11
DEWA	UNT to Toms Creek	10/8/2009	30	19	4	4	11	6	4.75	51.53	4.03	52.49
DEWA	UNT to Toms Creek	10/20/2010	23	11	3	3	5	4	17.72	81.77	3.84	22.58
DEWA	Mill Creek (DEWA)	10/6/2008	33	22	11	4	7	5	2.46	58.72	3.57	62.44
DEWA	Mill Creek (DEWA)	10/6/2009	34	23	7	7	9	6	1.80	65.23	3.56	64.20
DEWA	Mill Creek (DEWA)	10/20/2010	32	19	8	4	7	4	3.93	55.34	4.01	52.97
DEWA	Hornbecks Creek	10/6/2008	31	18	7	4	7	5	32.13	67.62	4.07	37.50
DEWA	Hornbecks Creek	10/5/2009	34	24	11	3	10	5	4.97	51.75	3.77	61.02
DEWA	Hornbecks Creek	10/20/2010	38	24	9	4	11	9	8.10	55.50	3.88	63.15
DEWA	Dingmans Creek	10/7/2008	26	14	4	3	7	8	57.74	80.97	4.90	27.18
DEWA	Dingmans Creek	10/6/2009	30	17	5	3	9	7	16.91	61.72	4.26	39.31
DEWA	Dingmans Creek	10/21/2010	34	22	7	4	11	5	49.09	64.02	4.51	35.16

Park[1]	Stream	Date	Taxa[2]	EPT[3]	E[4]	P[5]	T[6]	C-F[7]	%Non-insect[8]	%5 dominant[9]	MTI[10]	MIBI[11]
DEWA	Adams Creek	10/8/2008	37	25	8	6	11	8	1.12	59.81	3.49	70.21
DEWA	Adams Creek	10/5/2009	30	23	9	6	8	5	0.34	58.81	3.58	66.05
DEWA	Adams Creek	10/21/2010	32	23	11	5	7	4	6.19	70.43	3.49	55.26
DEWA	Raymondskill Creek	10/8/2008	37	20	9	4	7	6	10.71	40.36	4.37	55.25
DEWA	Raymondskill Creek	10/5/2009	37	23	7	4	12	9	4.83	53.78	4.29	60.11
DEWA	Raymondskill Creek	10/25/2010	38	18	7	3	8	7	3.87	46.10	4.10	59.90
DEWA	Spackmans Creek	10/6/2008	39	26	12	5	9	4	9.66	47.73	3.91	60.30
DEWA	Spackmans Creek	10/6/2009	32	23	8	8	7	3	4.19	60.53	3.75	62.46
DEWA	Spackmans Creek	10/20/2010	28	20	9	3	8	4	3.41	54.92	3.93	54.59
DEWA	Big Flat Brook	10/4/2008	36	17	7	2	8	7	5.59	65.17	3.79	53.91
DEWA	Big Flat Brook	10/6/2009	40	26	8	7	11	9	2.71	54.32	3.87	73.76
DEWA	Big Flat Brook	10/18/2010	39	24	7	6	11	7	2.67	60.24	3.70	64.77
DEWA	Shimers Brook	10/1/2008	26	12	2	2	8	6	1.31	82.73	4.38	40.38
DEWA	Shimers Brook	10/1/2009	24	14	3	2	9	6	0.87	63.49	4.03	49.98
DEWA	Shimers Brook	10/18/2010	28	15	2	1	12	7	1.31	71.98	4.06	48.38
DEWA	Little Flat Brook	10/4/2008	27	16	7	2	7	4	5.16	66.57	3.59	48.28
DEWA	Little Flat Brook	10/1/2009	31	17	4	3	10	5	2.26	67.47	4.47	41.51
DEWA	Little Flat Brook	10/18/2010	26	16	3	2	11	6	4.98	79.69	3.28	43.78
DEWA	Sawkill Creek	10/4/2008	33	22	9	5	8	4	0.03	71.31	3.34	56.97
DEWA	Sawkill Creek	10/9/2009	39	25	8	7	10	6	1.20	63.55	3.63	66.75
DEWA	Sawkill Creek	10/21/2010	40	24	12	5	7	4	5.44	64.40	3.88	57.63
DEWA	Bushkill Creek	10/7/2008	34	21	10	3	8	5	4.51	50.26	3.80	60.23
DEWA	Bushkill Creek	10/8/2009	39	25	9	5	11	8	15.53	52.66	3.94	57.98
DEWA	Bushkill Creek	10/25/2010	47	29	9	7	13	9	2.39	51.44	3.98	75.68
DEWA	Vandermark Creek	10/9/2008	31	20	5	6	9	5	9.24	49.04	3.67	56.72
DEWA	Vandermark Creek	10/5/2009	34	21	6	7	8	3	7.78	54.10	3.22	57.52
DEWA	Vandermark Creek	10/21/2010	37	24	7	7	10	5	2.53	52.80	3.39	66.11
DEWA	Flat Brook (Walpack)	10/1/2009	28	15	4	0	11	6	6.16	47.95	3.78	53.72
DEWA	Flat Brook (Walpack)	10/25/2010	33	18	5	2	11	6	4.30	60.21	3.89	50.91
DEWA	Flat Brook (Flatbrookville)	10/7/2009	40	25	9	2	14	9	2.19	63.91	3.73	64.87
DEWA	Flat Brook (Flatbrookville)	10/25/2010	35	20	5	2	13	7	4.82	61.33	3.72	53.62
JOFL	UNT to South Fork Little Conemaugh River	11/4/2008	18	7	1	1	5	4	0.56	84.97	5.38	23.61
JOFL	UNT to South Fork Little Conemaugh River	10/21/2009	24	8	1	3	4	5	2.92	82.90	5.09	23.82
JOFL	UNT to South Fork Little Conemaugh River	10/11/2010	28	9	2	2	5	6	8.60	78.66	5.54	22.23
UPDE	Shohola Creek	10/14/2008	34	22	5	4	13	9	3.00	73.75	3.85	54.84
UPDE	Shohola Creek	10/12/2009	40	25	7	5	13	9	2.96	63.45	3.74	64.94

Park[1]	Stream	Date	Taxa[2]	EPT[3]	E[4]	P[5]	T[6]	C-F[7]	%Non-insect[8]	%5 dominant[9]	MTI[10]	MIBI[11]
JPDE	Lackawaxen River	10/14/2008	40	27	9	7	11	8	9.48	59.93	4.25	62.33
JPDE	Lackawaxen River	10/12/2009	32	18	8	2	8	7	4.54	66.18	4.11	53.13
JPDE	Masthope Creek	10/14/2008	33	25	10	3	12	7	2.47	51.87	3.56	66.91
JPDE	Masthope Creek	10/12/2009	37	25	9	4	12	8	2.55	55.71	3.49	67.22
JPDE	Mongaup River	10/14/2008	40	30	8	4	18	11	8.75	60.15	3.58	64.38
JPDE	Mongaup River	10/12/2009	38	22	6	2	14	9	21.95	57.12	4.25	46.22
JPDE	Ten Mile River	10/15/2008	36	26	7	5	14	10	1.87	58.48	3.83	69.10
JPDE	Ten Mile River	10/12/2009	35	27	8	4	15	9	2.76	49.26	3.69	69.94
JPDE	Calkins Creek	10/15/2008	35	25	12	4	9	5	3.31	52.93	3.54	65.39
JPDE	Calkins Creek	10/13/2009	34	25	10	5	10	5	0.77	53.43	3.72	66.19
JPDE	Callicoon Creek	10/15/2008	35	26	11	5	10	6	0.03	55.28	3.68	70.06
JPDE	Callicoon Creek	10/13/2009	22	20	9	4	7	5	0.36	80.19	3.52	53.07
JPDE	Hankins Creek	10/15/2008	33	25	9	9	7	4	0.00	71.38	3.30	66.64
JPDE	Hankins Creek	10/13/2009	30	23	9	7	7	3	0.35	74.69	3.16	60.01
JPDE	Little Equinunk Creek	10/15/2008	35	23	7	7	9	6	1.47	69.05	3.38	63.02
JPDE	Little Equinunk Creek	10/14/2009	34	25	7	6	12	6	1.10	70.22	3.48	60.46
JPDE	East Branch Delaware River	10/16/2008	25	19	8	2	9	7	1.18	71.97	3.72	56.86
JPDE	East Branch Delaware River	10/13/2009	34	24	8	4	12	9	3.34	70.15	3.58	61.90
JPDE	Equinunk Creek	10/16/2008	38	25	9	7	9	6	1.15	53.66	3.81	70.62
JPDE	Equinunk Creek	10/14/2009	29	21	9	4	8	4	0.00	63.00	3.59	57.70
JPDE	West Branch Delaware River	10/27/2008	24	16	7	3	6	6	3.71	67.85	4.10	47.18
JPDE	West Branch Delaware River	11/19/2009	28	16	7	1	8	8	2.65	69.80	3.78	56.81

NPS 423/111731, 620/111731, 427/111731, 647/111731, December 2011

www.ingramcontent.com/pod-product-compliance
Lightning Source LLC
Chambersburg PA
CBHW080923290526
45795CB00007BA/2634

* 9 7 8 1 4 9 2 1 6 6 7 5 7 *